ceramicpainting
COLORWORKSHOP

ROCKPORT

First published in the United States of America by

Rockport Publishers, Inc.

33 Commercial Street

Gloucester, Massachusetts 01930-5089

Telephone: (978) 282-9590

Facsimile: (978) 283-2742

www.rockpub.com

ISBN 1-56496-755-7

10 9 8 7 6 5 4 3 2 1

Text by Livia McRee

Design: Leeann Leftwich

Cover Photography: Kevin Thomas

Printed in China.

GLOUCESTER MASSACHUSETTS

ROCKPORT PUBLISHERS

ceramicpainting

COLORWORKSHOP

PAINTS, PALETTES, AND PATTERNS FOR 16 PROJECTS

Doreen Mastandrea

Text by Livia McRee

CONTENTS

introduction

Painting on ceramics, unlike painting on canvas, presents the additional element of form. Certain colors and designs will accentuate particular ceramic forms, so making thoughtful choices when planning a project creates artful, as well as useful, ceramic pieces.

When planning a project, always keep in mind that ceramics are meant to be used. Consider how, where, and with what the piece will be used. Consider, for example, the time of day the piece will be used; whether it will stay indoors or outdoors;

and whether it will be used in a celebratory or reflective setting. Planning colors and designs accordingly will enhance the beauty of any piece.

Deciding how to use colors in painting can be overwhelming, given the wide variety of hues. Color preferences are, above all, personal, so when selecting a palette, consider the mood and feeling it evokes in you. The colors of each palette presented in this guide work together to convey a specific look and feel and offer a sure starting point.

Colors For Your Every Mood

FAVORITE BRIGHT COLORS

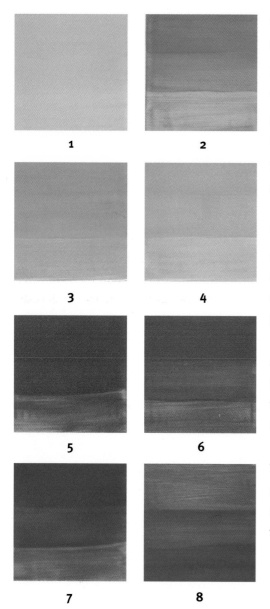

1 bright yellow

2 lime green

3 orange

4 honey yellow

5 apple red

6 deep orange

7 aquamarine

8 turquoise

The exciting colors of this palette lend the intensity of summer to a project. Sunny days, picnics, ripened fruit, and flowers bursting with color come to mind. Imagine a heap of tantalizing, vibrantly colored fruits...and a bowl large enough to accommodate the whole bunch! Red, ripe strawberries nestled in a turquoise or lime green bowl will look stunning and electrified.

A combination of colors from this palette—like orange, apple red, and lime green—can spark a traditional Mexican spirit. Pieces such as chip-n-dip plates, and platters that are intended to be used at gatherings, summertime celebrations, and parties look vibrant and festive when done in bright colors.

Wake up to these energizing colors! They can help start the day, making them the perfect choices for a coffee mug. The daily morning routine can also be a personal, reflective time. Try images on mugs that evoke a fond memory or a favorite hobby, to impart a cheery mood to the day or to spark creativity.

FAVORITE COOL COLORS

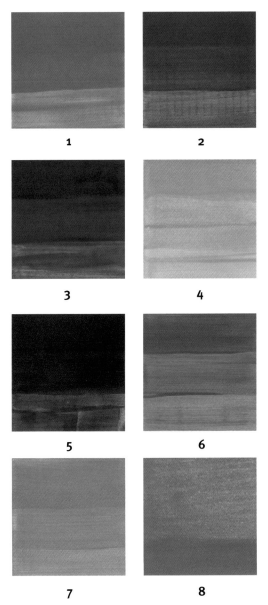

1   2

3   4

5   6

7   8

1 aqua

2 purple

3 royal blue

4 mint

5 deep blue-green

6 grape

7 light blue

8 turquoise

The range of cool colors evokes the many moods of the ocean and sky. Try using them on a seafood serving platter, or painting sea-life-inspired tiles to be placed in a shower or bathroom. The deep and light blues and greens in this palette also offer a lot of flexibility in depicting a wooded landscape, such as that on the bath set on page 44.

The temperament of this palette can range from serene and peaceful to serious and formal. Lighter colors such as mint, aqua, or light blue in a composition impart a calm, restful look. A predominance of darker colors like deep blue-green or royal blue lends a more reserved design.

Using exclusively blue tones on white ceramic pieces is a traditional decorative style in many countries. Used on a classical form such as a simple vase, this blue-and-white ware takes on an air of sophistication and history.

FAVORITE SOFT COLORS

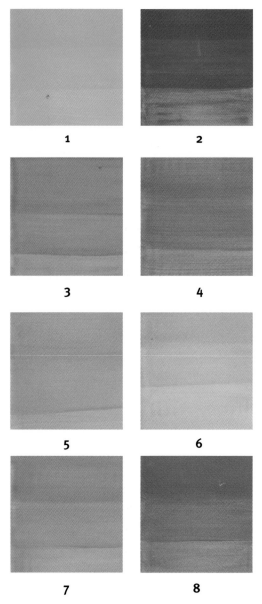

1 pale yellow

2 pink

3 peach

4 lavender

5 beige

6 light pink

7 mint

8 periwinkle

Soft colors are non-intrusive, so these are the colors to choose for a restful, soothing, and quiet setting.

Dessert plates showing off white frosted or powdered desserts look luscious, and a tea set for one invites quiet contemplation. A light switch like the one on page 70 blends easily into a room's décor and adds a creative accent against a white wall.

The muted look of soft colors can also create a feeling of age or antiquity. Think of a faded frescoed wall or a sun-bleached outdoor mural. To recreate this feeling, try sponging or layering paints for a variegated depth of color.

TIP: When sponging colors it is best to use colors of similar intensity so they blend well together. Avoid using very dark colors with very light colors—the light colors will get lost.

FAVORITE EARTH COLORS

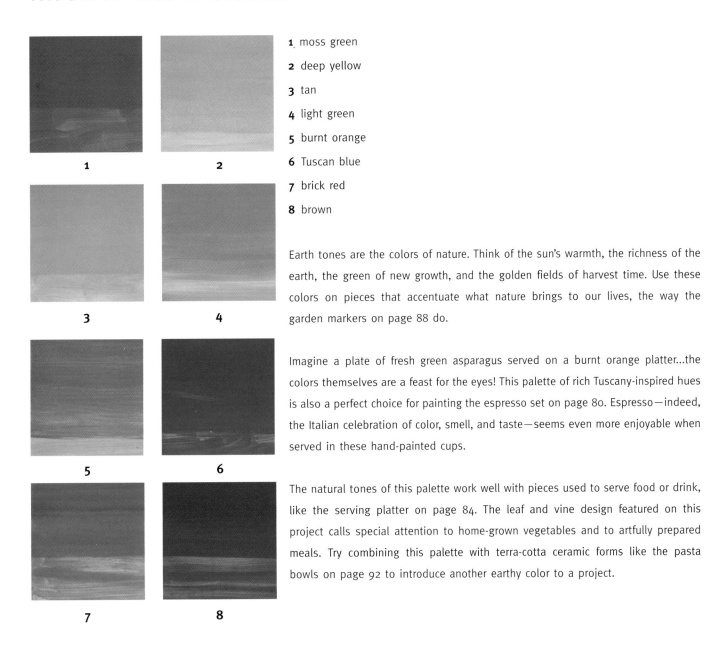

1 moss green

2 deep yellow

3 tan

4 light green

5 burnt orange

6 Tuscan blue

7 brick red

8 brown

Earth tones are the colors of nature. Think of the sun's warmth, the richness of the earth, the green of new growth, and the golden fields of harvest time. Use these colors on pieces that accentuate what nature brings to our lives, the way the garden markers on page 88 do.

Imagine a plate of fresh green asparagus served on a burnt orange platter...the colors themselves are a feast for the eyes! This palette of rich Tuscany-inspired hues is also a perfect choice for painting the espresso set on page 80. Espresso—indeed, the Italian celebration of color, smell, and taste—seems even more enjoyable when served in these hand-painted cups.

The natural tones of this palette work well with pieces used to serve food or drink, like the serving platter on page 84. The leaf and vine design featured on this project calls special attention to home-grown vegetables and to artfully prepared meals. Try combining this palette with terra-cotta ceramic forms like the pasta bowls on page 92 to introduce another earthy color to a project.

The colors of this palette uplift like a field of vibrant summer-blooming flowers or a harvest of fresh fruits—lemons, limes, apples, and oranges. These engaging hues don't hide...they entice you to participate, making them the natural choices for celebrating, entertaining, or gathering informally with friends and family.

favorite**bright**colors

When you want to perk up a bland room or add cheer to your home, choose one or a combination of these colors. Since they energize their surroundings, try them on coffee mugs and cereal bowls for the perfect pick-me-up in the breakfast nook. For entertaining, a party platter painted with these colors adds festivity to a gathering and invitingly displays whatever is being served.

Since these bold colors speak for themselves, simple designs such as stripes or other geometric patterns are a perfect match. Outlining designs in black makes the colors pop even more. Anything can be transformed into an eye-catching centerpiece when accented with this dramatic palette. The playful, primary feel they impart also works well in children's rooms or any space calling for a whimsical touch.

illustrated MUGS

MATERIALS

- **#3 or #4 round brush**
- **thin liner brush**
- **masking tape**
- **pencil**
- **ceramic paint underglaze colors: lime green, deep orange, black**

Here, a single bright background color calls attention to the crisp, modern, black-and-white designs on these mugs rather than competes with them. A whole set, each painted with a different bright hue, energizes the breakfast table no matter what you're drinking. Try designing the motifs for each mug around a central theme such as geometric shapes, letters, or numbers.

STARTING OUT
Masking tape creates quick, perfect templates for the rectangles and stripes on these mugs. When drawing small-scale designs, avoid adding details. Keep the designs simple to create maximum impact.

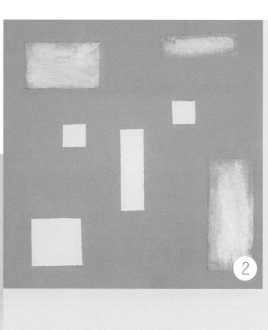

STEP 1 Pencil in two lines about ¼" (.5 cm) apart just under the lip of the mug. Draw one line on the inside of the cup about as far down as the bottom line on the outside. Tape equally spaced stripes on the handles of the mug. Cut a few rectangles of varying sizes from the tape and apply them randomly around the mug.

STEP 2 Paint three coats of deep orange or lime green on the mug under the bottom pencil lines, inside and out, excluding the handle. Let each coat dry completely before applying the next one. Remove the tape from the mug once it has dried. If any paint has bled under the taped areas, carefully scrape it away using a craft knife.

tip
If you find it awkward to tape the handle and you don't have difficulty staying within the lines when you paint, try drawing the stripes freehand in pencil.

tip

Keep line drawings simple. They are easy to paint and are bold rather than busy.

VARIATION

Wide, alternating stripes of color are vivid enough to stand alone. Here, the linear design is maintained by continuing the stripes to the handle.

Pencil in two lines about $\frac{1}{4}$" (.5 cm) apart just under the lip of the mug. Below them, draw two lines around the mug to create three equal sections. Draw two lines around the handle to create a visually continuous stripe pattern. Apply three coats of deep orange on the inside of the mug, continuing outward to the second line under the lip. In each of the remaining striped areas, apply three coats of one color. Bright yellow, aquamarine, and lime green were used for the stripes on this mug. Using a thin liner brush, paint over pencil lines with one coat of black.

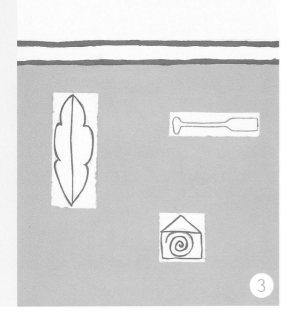

STEP 3 Pencil in designs in each of the white rectangles created by the tape. Using a thin liner brush, paint over all pencil lines with one coat of black. Any pencil lines that remain visible will burn off in the kiln. Paint around the taped stripes on the handle with one coat of black. Remove the tape. If necessary, scrape away excess paint with a craft knife, or add paint with a small brush to ensure crisp lines. Patterns for this project can be found on page 102.

DEEP ORANGE

BRIGHT YELLOW

AQUAMARINE

LIME GREEN

salt & pepper SHAKERS

These nature-themed shakers will add a touch of whimsy to the table. A matching set is created not only by using related motifs, but also by repeating the same three colors in both shakers. The leaves are a combination of bright yellow and lime green with a background of apple red, while the flowers are bright yellow and apple red with a background of lime green. A simple shift in the dominant color makes each shaker unique but harmonious.

MATERIALS

- #3 or #4 round brush
- thin liner brush
- pencil
- ceramic paint underglaze colors: lime green, bright yellow, apple red, black

STARTING OUT To transfer designs more easily to a curved surface, try cutting the tracing pattern out of adhesive vinyl. It can be easily removed from or repositioned on ceramic surfaces.

STEP 1 Cut out the leaf template on page 103 and trace the pattern randomly around the shaker with a pencil. Then draw a line down the center of each leaf. Cut out the flower template on page 103 and trace this pattern randomly around the other shaker with a pencil.

STEP 2 Paint each leaf with two coats of lime green. Paint one coat of bright yellow over half of each leaf. Let each coat dry completely before applying the next one. Paint each flower with two coats of bright yellow. When completely dry, dip the handle end of your brush in apple red and make a dot in the center of each flower. Use enough paint on the handle end to create a solid dot. Too little paint will cause unevenly colored, incomplete, or translucent dots after firing.

tip

With a little practice, you can draw simple patterns, such as these, freehand to save time.

VARIATION

This shaker incorporates a traditional Italian scroll pattern, reminiscent of a curving vine.

Draw the leaves on the shaker as indicated in step 1 of the main projecte. Draw a freehand wave pattern around the neck of the shaker with a line above and below it. Paint the leaves as indicated. Paint the entire background except for the neck of the shaker with three coats of turquoise. Paint the wave pattern with apple red and green. Here, equal parts bright yellow and turquoise were mixed to create a new green. Using a thin liner brush, outline the wave pattern and the leaves with one coat of black. Also paint the scroll pattern in black. Finally, paint dots of apple red at the curled end of each scroll.

STEP 3 Paint the remaining areas of the leaf shaker with three coats of brick red, carefully avoiding the leaves. Let each coat dry completely before applying the next one. Using a thin liner brush, outline and paint a line down the middle of each leaf with one coat of black. Paint the remaining areas of the flower shaker with three coats of lime green, carefully avoiding the flowers. Outline the flowers, including the center circle, with one coat of black.

LIME GREEN

BRIGHT YELLOW

APPLE RED

TURQUOISE

chip 'n dip
PARTY PLATTER

This feisty platter is sure to add a festive air to any party or gathering. Bright colors and free-form designs work together to create an energetic, informal mood. To create this design, adhesive vinyl was cut and adhered to the painted platter, making it easy to neatly paint the second color around the pattern. If the paint is completely dry, the vinyl won't damage it when removed.

MATERIALS

- #3 or #4 round brush
- thin liner brush
- adhesive vinyl
- pencil
- ceramic paint underglaze colors: lime green, bright yellow, apple red, turquoise, white, black

STARTING OUT
To make the abstract designs on this platter, sketch and cut out the design on paper first and adjust it as necessary. When you are happy with the pattern, trace it with a permanent marker on a piece of adhesive vinyl.

STEP 1 Paint one outer segment of the plate and the center with two coats of bright yellow. Paint another segment with two coats of lime green. Paint the final segment with two coats of turquoise. Be sure to leave the dividers and outer edge of the plate unpainted for now. Draw abstract designs freehand on adhesive vinyl, cut them out, and adhere them to the bottom of each outer segment. Make sure the paint is completely dry before trying to adhere the vinyl, or the adhesive won't stick.

STEP 2 Apply two coats of lime green over the bright yellow; two coats of turquoise over the lime green; and two coats of bright yellow over the turquoise. After each two applications, remove the vinyl when the paint is dry. Paint a circle of turquoise around the center section, leaving the middle yellow. Paint an apple red spiral in the yellow center.

tip
To create an outlined design like the one seen here in the green segment, simply cut out the center of the vinyl, roughly following the outer shape.

tip

If any paint has bled underneath the vinyl, gently scrape it away with a craft knife. Then, with a thin liner brush touch up the edges of the patterns to create a crisp edge where there may have been color bleeding.

STEP 3 Paint the outer edge, the underside of the plate, and the dividers of the plate with one generous coat of black. When the paint is completely dry, dip the handle end of your brush in white and dab dots of varying sizes all over the outer edge of the plate. The variation in dot size makes for a more intersting and active border. Use enough paint on the handle end to create a solid dot. Too little paint will cause unevenly colored, incomplete, or translucent dots after firing.

variation

VARIATION

This plate is a fun way to present tortilla chips and salsa. Begin by painting the outer segments with three coats of apple red, orange, and deep orange as seen here. Using the template on page 105, draw a chili pepper in the center of the plate and paint the top lime green and the bottom apple red. Carefully outline the pepper in black, leaving a scalloped edge. Paint the dividers and center just to the scalloped edge with three coats of lime green. When the paint is completely dry, dip the handle end of your brush in apple red and mark a dot within each scallop of the border. Paint the outer edge with lime green and honey yellow stripes, alternating the widths as seen here. Outline the stripes with black.

LIME GREEN

ORANGE

HONEY YELLOW

APPLE RED

DEEP ORANGE

fruit
PLATES

Sgraffito is an ancient ceramic carving technique that enables you to draw designs in paint. In this project, contrasting colors are layered, and a leaf pattern is carved into the top coat to reveal the black base coat. For maximum impact, the base coat must be solid and opaque. At least two top layers of paint are needed so that the top color remains distinct. In this case, three top layers of paint are used since the base coat is black.

MATERIALS

- #3 or #4 round brush
- thin liner brush
- ceramic paint underglaze colors: apple red, lime green, honey yellow, white, black

STARTING OUT Practice the sgraffito technique on a tile first. The final coat of paint should be wet, but not too wet, when carving the outline of the leaf. If it is too dry, the paint will chip off, leaving a messy look to the line.

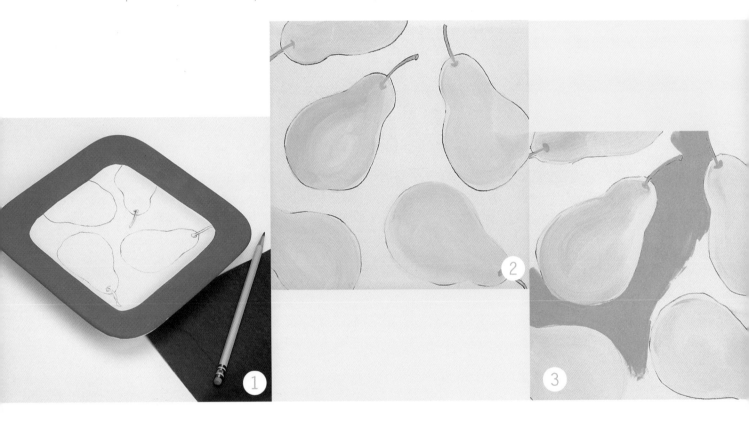

STEP 1 Transfer the pear design from page 104 several times to the center of the plate by using graphite paper or by tracing a cutout pear with a pencil. Arrange the pears in a random pattern, with some of the pears partially hidden by the edge of the plate. Paint the edge of the plate with two coats of black.

STEP 2 Paint the pears with one coat of honey yellow. While the paint is still wet, highlight the edges of the pears with a small amount of apple red, making sure the colors are well blended. See "Blending Colors" in the Earth Colors Workshop on page 97. Next, mix an equal amount of apple red and honey yellow to create the brown color for the stems. Paint the stems with two coats of the brown using a liner brush.

STEP 3 Paint around the pears with three coats of apple red. Let each coat dry completely before applying the next one. With a thin liner brush, outline the pears and stems with one coat of black. At the base of each stem, make the outline slightly thicker to suggest an indentation.

tips

To paint other fruit, such as the cherries seen in this project, use the same techniques as used for the pears, but be sure to pick background colors that will make the fruit stand out.

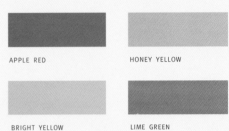

VARIATION 1 To make this fruit bowl, use the same techniques described for the plate, but for the lemons paint over a bright yellow base coat with honey yellow, leaving some small areas of bright yellow as highlights. Using a thin liner brush, outline the lemons with one coat of black, and randomly add tiny dots to suggest a dimpled surface. Paint the black border on the outside of the bowl, and mix equal parts of apple red and white paint to create the lighter shade of the bowl's exterior.

APPLE RED

HONEY YELLOW

BRIGHT YELLOW

LIME GREEN

(4)

STEP 4 Paint oval shapes around the edge of the plate with one coat of white and let dry completely. Next, paint two coats of lime green over the white ovals. Let the first coat dry completely. While the second coat is still wet, take the end of a brush or a dull pencil and scrape the leaf outline into the paint so that the black base coat is revealed. Use a soft brush to remove any excess paint; wait until the piece is dry to avoid damaging the sgrafitto lines. See "Successful Sgraffito" in the Bright Colors Workshop on page 32.

VARIATION 2 With the plate at a diagonal, draw two lines to divide the space into three approximately equal parts. Then draw two more lines equally spaced and perpendicular to the first set of lines. Paint the sections with three coats of deep orange, lime green, and aquamarine as seen here. Finally, paint the lines between the sections with black.

DEEP ORANGE

AQUAMARINE

LIME GREEN

favoritebrightcolors
Color and Painting Workshop

choosing the right brush

Using the appropriate brushes for a project is essential to successful painting. The right brush for a particular process makes each step much easier and allows you to focus on your designs. Available in a wide variety of shapes and sizes, brushes can be the key to achieving a desired look or executing an intricate design.

When selecting brushes, begin by experimenting with their capabilities. Try loading the brush with various amounts of paint, brushing quickly or slowly, and twisting or turning the brush as you paint to discover what types of lines and strokes you can get. You can even use the blunt ends of some brushes to create perfectly round dots or to etch out intricate designs (see "Successful Sgrafitto" page 32). Since the blunt end of some brushes is not as sharp as that of a pencil, wider lines are possible. Use damaged or broken bisque (once-fired, unglazed ceramic ware) to experiment on, or an absorbent paper to simulate the surface of bisque.

Many specialty brushes are designed to produce unique and unusual effects that can add another dimension to your work. While most studios will have a variety of brushes available to use, buying a personal set ensures that you will always have the ones you like on hand and in good condition.

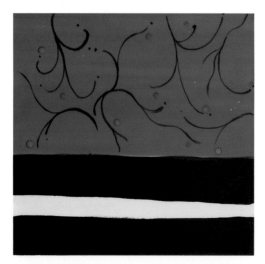

A wide brush is best used to paint bold, graphic lines or to quickly cover an area with paint, while a liner brush is key to painting a delicate design, as well as to outlining. The dots on this tile were made with the blunt end of a brush.

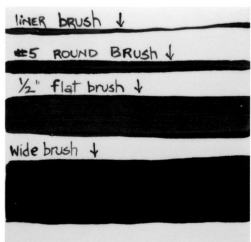

A basic painting set should include liner, round, flat, and wide brushes. Each is designed to produce a specific type of line easily.

using black and white

Bright colors are inherently vibrant, but when contrasted with black, they will appear even more so. White can also serve the same purpose, especially when used with black, as in the Chip-n-Dip Party Platter project on page 22.

One way to easily incorporate black into your designs is to outline them. A black outline accentuates central motifs by making them appear to pop out of the background. The outline should be thick or thin depending on the design. For example, large or simple shapes demand a thicker outline whereas small, intricate, or delicate shapes require a thinner outline.

Don't worry about painting black over bright colors. In contrast to the usual three or four coats necessary for any other hue, one good coat of black is all that is necessary for a solid black line, even when it is layered over other colors.

These stripes of color from the bright palette have an energetic appeal, especially when used together.

When contrasted with black dividing lines, each color appears even brighter and seems to pop out from the piece.

When white is added to a bright color, the result is a softer hue that can be used to subtly accent or shade the original color.

successful sgraffito

Sgraffito is a technique that has been used by potters for centuries. Initially, red clay forms were painted entirely with white paint, and designs were scratched into the paint to reveal the color of the clay beneath. Intricate designs with thin lines are made possible with sgraffito. As a result, this technique makes it very easy to incorporate words or messages into your work.

This technique can also be applied to layers of paint. For maximum impact, choose colors that boldly contrast with each other so that the design will be very visible. Use at least three coats of paint for the base color and at least two for the top color. However, for a black base, you will only need two coats of base paint. To keep the top color from being muddied by the black beneath it, start with one coat of white paint over the black, followed by two coats of the top color.

Make sure the base color paint is completely dry before adding the top color. This prevents the colors from blending. To ensure unbroken etched lines, however, scratch designs in the top color before it is completely dry. The paint will dry in only a few minutes. Be careful not to scratch so deeply as to scrape away the base coat. A pencil makes the perfect etching tool for sgraffito, but experimenting with different items such as a pottery needle, a paperclip, a toothpick, woodcarving tools, or the blunt end of a paintbrush is sure to lead to some interesting discoveries! Be sure to have a soft brush on hand to whisk away the paint scrapings.

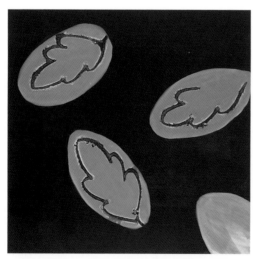

The top layer of paint on this tile was too dry at the time of scratching, thus resulting in the broken lines seen here. The paint flaked off randomly around the etching.

Etch lines just as the paint begins to dry to get the smooth, flowing lines seen here.

stenciling and masking

Stencils make it possible to paint designs that call for steady lines—including ornate ones—with confidence, relative ease, and speed. Use plastic, store-bought stencils, or try tracing an image on adhesive vinyl and cutting along the outline with a craft knife to make an easy-to-use, non-damaging version. You can also use adhesive vinyl cutouts as reverse-stencils, painting around the stencil rather than within it.

If applying an adhesive vinyl stencil over paint, be sure to position it when the paint is completely dry so that it will stick properly. Although the stencil provides clean edges for your design, try to avoid going over the edges of the adhesive vinyl to prevent paint from seeping under it. This also helps to prevent the paint from cracking when the stencil is removed. When the top coat of paint is dry, carefully peel away the stencil. If paint has seeped underneath the stencil, use a craft knife to gently scrape away the unwanted color and to clean up the edges of the design. If necessary, use a thin liner brush to touch up any damaged paint.

tip

When using plastic stencils, simply trace the image with a #2 pencil, on either an unpainted or painted surface. Use the lines as guides, but don't worry about covering or erasing them; they will burn off when the piece is fired.

Paint around the adhesive vinyl so that it is easily removed and doesn't cause the surrounding paint to flake off.

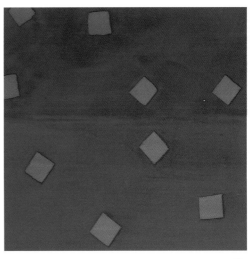

The crisp lines necessary for these squares are easily attained with stencils. The lines would be quite challenging to paint without the stencils.

Stormy or calm, bold or subtle, this palette is multifaceted. It can evoke the many moods of the sea, a peaceful day in winter, the coziness of a seaside cottage, or an air of reserved elegance.

favorite**cool**colors

Since aquatic motifs are the perfect match for this palette, try painting some sea-life-inspired accent tiles for your tub or shower, where a bit of the ocean fits right in. To capture the ever-changing face of the sea, blending and sponging several different colors together is an effective impressionistic technique. To suggest water in a bolder, more abstract way, try breaking up the surface to be painted with curving lines, and coloring the resulting areas with different hues.

A ceramic bath set painted with these serene shades can add a bit of sky and faraway vistas. You can also create elegantly striking pieces that recall classic blue-and-white ware by using the darker shades of this palette contrasted with white motifs.

stamped SEA TILES

Cool colors are the key to creating the aquatic complexion of these tiles. A background wash of color lends an ocean feel. The realistic motifs are stamped on the tiles, giving the impression of a detailed, framed print with relative ease.

MATERIALS

- #3 or #4 round brush
- thin liner brush
- pencil
- fish stamp
- ceramic paint underglaze colors: light blue, royal blue, deep blue-green, aqua, black

STARTING OUT Both flexible foam and rubber stamps can be used with ceramic paints. Be sure to do a test stamping on a piece of paper first to see how much paint is necessary.

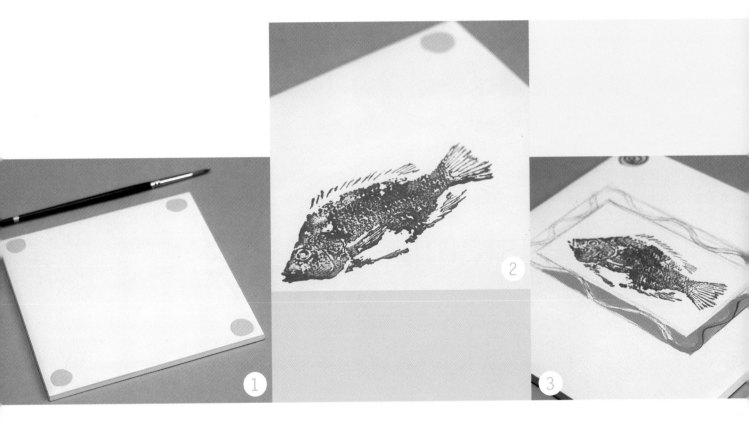

STEP 1 Paint the tile with one coat of light blue. Paint a dot in each corner, about the size of a dime, with one coat of aqua.

STEP 2 Brush an even coat of black paint on the stamp. Center the stamp on the tile and apply firm, even pressure.

STEP 3 With a pencil, draw a frame around the stamp. Paint the frame with one coat of royal blue. When it is completely dry, paint a freehand scalloped border in the frame with 2 coats of deep blue-green. See page 106 for patterns.

VARIATION 1: This scrolling vine design works well independently. However, it becomes more intriguing when several of these tiles are placed next to each other as a bathroom backsplash. Paint a thin wash of light blue over the entire tile. Brush a coat of black paint on the stamp and press in the center of the tile. Draw a rectangular frame around the fish. Paint the inside of the frame with one coat of royal blue. Draw a freehand scroll within the confines of the frame border and paint it deep blue-green. Draw a larger scrolling vine pattern around the inside edge as shown in the template on page 108. Paint with a mix of deep blue-green and royal blue. Outline the frame, the inner scroll, and the outer scroll with one coat of black using a thin liner brush.

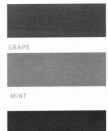

GRAPE

MINT

ROYAL BLUE

LINDA MASTANDREA

VARIATION 2: Conjure up your own whimsical creatures based on the unusual shapes and expressive eyes and mouths of sea animals or use the template on page 106. Pencil in animals and abstract shapes to suggest water. Paint the animals with one coat of mint, leaving the lips and eyes unpainted. Paint the abstract shapes with one thin coat of grape to achieve the translucent effect, and paint two heavy coats of royal blue to achieve the darker, opaque effect. Try using other color combinations such as aqua and deep blue-green for a bolder effect. Outline the animals and paint dots for the eyes in black.

STEP 4 Using a thin liner brush, paint spirals in the corner circles with one coat of black. Outline the frame and scalloped border with black.

two-tone
BOTTLE VASE

This vase is reminiscent of the blue-and-white ware found throughout the history of world ceramics, from Ming vases to Wedgwood dinnerware. Two subtly different shades of blue add depth to the design and accentuate the voluptuous base, while the repeating graphic pattern creates a modern look. Experiment with the size of the flowers to see the variety of effects that can be achieved from a simple change in size. For example, a multitude of tiny flowers has a much daintier feel than a few large '70s-style blossoms. Use the templates on page 109 as guides.

MATERIALS

- #0 or #1 and #5 or #6 round brushes
- thin liner brush
- ceramic paint underglaze colors: royal blue; deep blue-green; light blue; yellow for flower centers

STARTING OUT

The beauty and appeal of this vase lie in its luscious, rich color. Apply at least three solid, even coats of paint so that brush strokes are minimal.

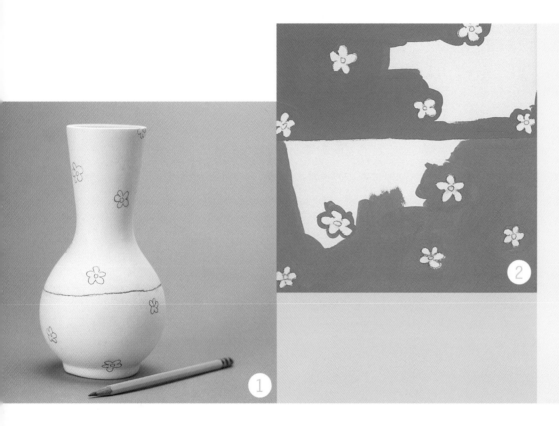

STEP 1 Draw a line around the vase about two-thirds of the way down from the top with a pencil. Draw freehand flowers, or transfer the flower from the pattern on page 109 randomly around the vase.

STEP 2 Paint the top part of the vase with at least three coats of royal blue, carefully avoiding the flowers. In the same manner, paint the bottom half of the vase with three coats of deep blue-green.

tip

To paint around the flowers easily, use a small round brush such as a #0 or #1 and only cover the area immediately surrounding each flower. Then, paint the remaining areas of the vase with a #5 or #6 round brush.

STEP 3 Using a thin liner brush, add accent lines to the petals and outline the inner circle of the flowers with pale blue. With the blunt end of a brush, dab a dot of yellow in the center of each flower.

VARIATION 1

Follow step 1 of the main project, but transfer the tri-leaf pattern from page 116 to the lower one-third of the vase. Paint the top of the vase as indicated in the main project. On the lower section, paint the leaves with one or two coats of mint or pale yellow. Let them dry completely. Using a thin liner brush, outline the leaves and add veins in black.

ROYAL BLUE

LIGHT BLUE

MINT

PALE YELLOW

VARIATION 2

The vase seen here has a more classic blue-and-white ware look. Follow the directions for the main project, but paint the entire vase with royal blue and choose larger flowers.

ROYAL BLUE

LIGHT BLUE
YELLOW FOR FLOWER CENTERS

CERAMICS COURTESY OF VALERIA LANZA

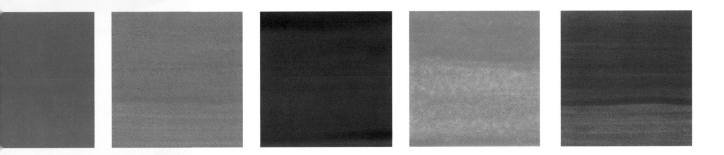

landscape
BATHROOM SET

MATERIALS

- #4 or #5 round brush
- sea sponges or silk sponges
- ceramic paint underglaze colors: aqua; light blue; royal blue; mint; grape

A bathroom always feels more comfortably intimate and relaxing when filled with blues and greens. This decorative but utilitarian set is sure to earn the admiration of guests and conjure up visions of beautiful, natural vistas. Painted in part with sponges, simple suggestive shapes and layers of paint are used to convey a moody sky and a forest scene. Experiment with the different types of sponges available at art and craft supply stores; try cutting them into specialized shapes to further refine the basic sponging technique. (See "Sponging" page 76.)

STARTING OUT

To successfully create an impressionistic landscape using sponging techniques, don't be afraid to wipe away paint or add additional layers. Since the loose style of this design makes a pattern impractical, use these directions for inspiration and guidance—experiment on a tile first, until you achieve the feeling of a landscape.

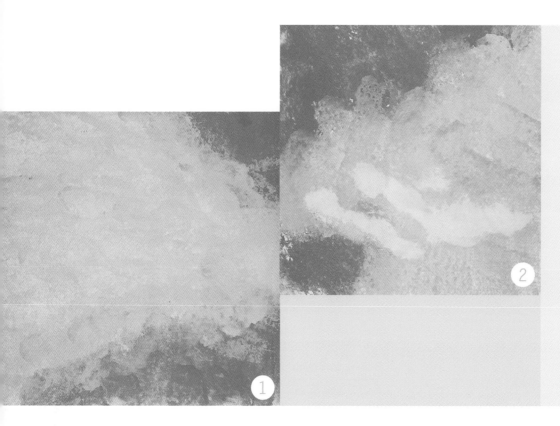

STEP 1 Sponge the entire surface of the cup, soap dish, and toothbrush holder with light blue. Using royal blue and then grape, sponge small areas of the sky and define a "ground line," which will determine where to begin sponging the bottom of the trees. Since royal blue and grape are the darkest colors used in this project, they are the most effective in visually separating the sky and the ground.

STEP 2 Using a clean sponge and water, wipe all the way down to the white clay body to create clouds. Don't worry about wiping off too much because more paint can be sponged on later.

VARIATION

Try adding another dimension to the landscape by applying the sgrafitto technique described on page 32. Use a blunt pencil tip or the end of a brush to carve accent strokes that will add movement and vitality to your trees.

STEP 3 With aqua, create trees with a #4 or #5 round brush, using short dabs for brush strokes. Lightly brush over some of the aqua with mint to add highlights and depth to the foliage. Finally, shade the ground area around the bases of the trees using royal blue and grape.

AQUA

LIGHT BLUE

ROYAL BLUE

MINT

GRAPE

fishbone
PLATTER

An oval platter was chosen to emphasize the elongated shape of this stylized fish skeleton. When a design, such as this one, demands a central motif that is solidly and evenly black, two coats of black are recommended. To properly contrast this dark, bold design, three heavy coats of paint were necessary to achieve maximum color intensity for the background and edge of the platter.

PLATTER

STARTING OUT Be sure to select a ceramic form that can be proportionately filled by the fish skeleton. If necessary, adjust the overall size of the pattern to better fit the space.

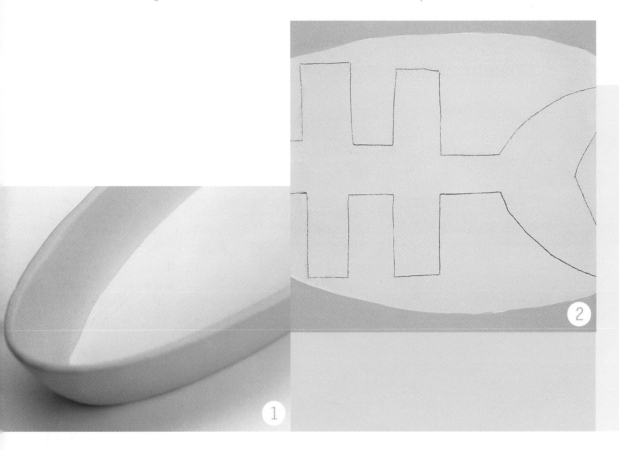

STEP 1 Using a wide, flat brush, apply three coats of mint to the bottom of the platter. Apply three coats of grape to the rim and the underside of the platter. Let each coat dry completely before applying the next one.

STEP 2 Transfer the fish skeleton pattern on page 107 to the inside bottom of the platter.

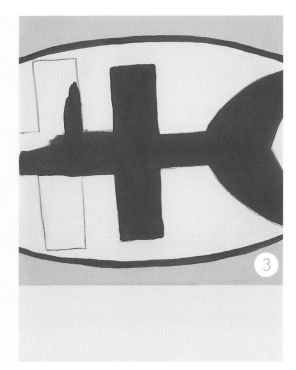

STEP 3 Fill in the fish with two coats of black for solid, even coverage. Outline with black the edge of the platter and the bottom where the mint and grape sections meet.

VARIATION

Transfer the wave border pattern on page 108 to the edge of the platter. Paint the inside of the platter just to the edge of the border pattern with two coats of light blue. Paint the border and the underside of the platter with three coats of royal blue. Let each coat dry completely before applying the next one. Next, transfer the starfish pattern on page 108 to the platter. Try adding a number of starfish of varying sizes. Mix equal parts light blue and royal blue, and paint the starfish with one coat of the mixture. With a thin liner brush, outline and add details to the starfish, as illustrated here, with royal blue.

LIGHT BLUE   ROYAL BLUE

favorite**cool**colors
Color and Painting Workshop

painting
water & sky

Blending, layering, and combining the blue, green, and purple hues of this palette can't fail to capture the ever-changing essence of sea and sky. To help refine the style needed to depict a particular mood, experiment with different tools, such as brushes of various sizes, and techniques, such as sponging.

When painting water, using at least two colors can help capture natural tonal variations. Blending the colors together (see "Blending Colors" page 97) softens the transition between different hues and lends a more realistic look. Use a wet brush and apply successive layers of paint before the previous one has dried. For a stylized or abstract suggestion of water, consider curving interlocked shapes as used for the whimsical tile variation on page 39.

When painting a sky, use the same methods as described for painting water. Just add clouds. To create soft, natural clouds, paint the entire sky, then wipe the paint away down to the bare clay surface. Also, try cutting a cloud shape out of adhesive vinyl and painting around it. The shape of the clouds will be sharply defined, resulting in a more graphic look.

Thin coats of turquoise and aqua are swirled back and forth to create the fluid effect seen here. Blend the colors as you apply them to the piece and use long, flowing brush strokes.

This tile was painted with mint, but the brush was dipped in water while painting to achieve the softened, variegated look. Use this technique to project a calm, subtle feeling.

Royal blue, light blue, and aqua were applied in sequence and then wiped away to create the clouds seen here. A small, synthetic craft sponge works best.

stamping

Stamping is a quick and easy way to add details to a painting, and the process can be mastered quickly with just a bit of practice. Since stamps allow a design to be precisely replicated from project to project, try painting a set of dishes unified by a special motif or a "signature" stamp.

Very detailed rubber stamps allow beginners to incorporate intricate designs into a project. Try stamping in one color and adding accents with a fine brush to add even more detail, as well as to personalize the image. Soft foam stamps, available at craft supply stores, are generally much less detailed. The result is a much simpler look, perfect for creating repeating patterns like a checkerboard or a border.

At first, it may be difficult to adjust the amount of paint needed on a stamp to get a clear, complete impression, especially when working with intricate rubber stamps. Use a brush to apply an even coat of paint to the stamp, and always do a test stamp first on a piece of broken, unfired pottery or absorbent paper. The amount of pressure applied when stamping the image will also affect the result. Use firm, even pressure, but do not press too hard or the paint will become rippled. Finally, use a small brush to touch up any bare areas or remove any excess paint.

This tile shows the effect of too much paint (top), just enough paint, and too little paint (bottom) on a stamp.

blue-and-white ware

Blue-and-white ware can be found throughout the history of ceramics and in many parts of the world. Porcelain ware with this style of decoration, the kind typical of Chinese and English pottery, is decorated by painting designs with a material called cobalt oxide. In Mexico and Italy, ceramic pieces are decorated with cobalt oxide to achieve a deep, rich blue over a white base-glaze. Italian pottery of this kind is called *Majolica;* the Mexican version is referred to as *Puebla.*

The cool colors of this palette are perfect for creating blue-and-white-ware-inspired pottery. A visit to a museum or gallery or a look through art books will yield a variety of classic ideas that can't help but inspire a personal version of this decorative style.

English and Chinese blue-and-white ware generally depict elaborate or intricate scenes. Try using intricate stamps to replicate this style or combine hand-painted designs with stamping. Mexican blue-and-white ware features simpler, more graphic designs that are equally as inspiring and impressive.

Traditionally, cobalt oxide was mixed with different amounts of a white colorant, usually a glaze or underglaze, to get a range of colors from light blue to dark blue. In addition to mixing white and blue underglazes to achieve this effect, try adding water to thin blue paint for a faded look.

Most blue-and-white ware has a tonal range from light to dark, as illustrated in these further examples of blue-and-white ware designs.

color opacity & mixing

Opaque blue tones are typically harder to achieve than other opaque colors. When you use a light shade of blue, one thin coat of paint can end up being hardly noticeable, whereas with most other colors the result would be light and translucent but still visible. Take this into consideration when planning a project, and paint a test tile to determine how many coats will be necessary to achieve the desired results.

Since blues need to be applied more heavily to get an opaque color, brush strokes will be more visible as well, so it doesn't hurt to apply an extra layer of paint to minimize this, if desired. Another option is to take advantage of these qualities rather than to overcome them. Planning a design around these constraints can lead to an inspired, interesting design!

Finally, since all the colors of this palette are closely related, color mixing is an easy way to create subtly different colors that add depth and dimension to a project.

Royal blue and aqua were mixed in equal proportions to elicit the slate blue color in the middle. Creating new colors this way provides an infinite variety of shades that expand the palette.

Mint and turquoise were mixed in equal proportions to make the baby blue color in the middle. When freely experimenting with color mixing, unexpected results can be very rewarding!

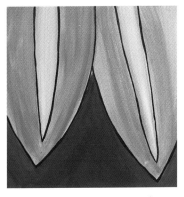

This tile shows how opaque colors and translucent colors can work together. The leaves seem more lively and fluid against the solid background.

The tile seen here shows one, two, and three coats of royal blue. Be sure to use at least three thick, even coats for a deep, opaque color.

Deep blue-green is shown here as an example of one, two, and three layers of paint. While opacity may be desirable for some projects, a wash of color may be just the right touch for others.

The muted colors of this palette have the appeal of spring's first buds... new, fresh, and delicate. Pastels subtly invite you to slow down and enjoy the quiet pleasures of life, like a cup of tea and a good book. These are the colors to surround yourself with when you want to retreat and relax.

favorite**soft**colors

Since soft colors easily blend into their surroundings, use them in your home to paint decorative accents such as switch plate covers that can add a subtle charm without detracting from other elements in a room. For the times when you need to unwind, try tea for one served in a nestled pot and cup painted in these soothing hues. For an intimate gathering of two or three, a special treat seems a bit tastier when served on daintily painted dessert plates.

When layered, and especially when sponged, these colors will lend an impression-istic feel to a design, making it easy to conjure up the dreamy world of a Monet painting. Use these hues on anything for an infant's room, a bedroom—anywhere a peaceful atmosphere is welcome.

nestled
TEAPOT & CUP

This nestled tea-for-one set presents a unique design opportunity. Consider how each piece will look both separately and together while transferring the pattern. For this intimate ceramic form, a relaxed, washed effect was created by painting just two coats of an uplifting pastel yellow. The illusion of unused tea bags is created using a realistic light beige. As a variation, try painting the words on the tags in lowercase or script.

MATERIALS

- #3 or #4 round brush
- thin liner brush
- ceramic paint underglaze colors: pale yellow, beige, mint, periwinkle, peach, black

STARTING OUT Be sure to nestle the pot, lid, and cup together before transferring the pattern. Both handles should be aligned as well, to ensure the continuity of the design.

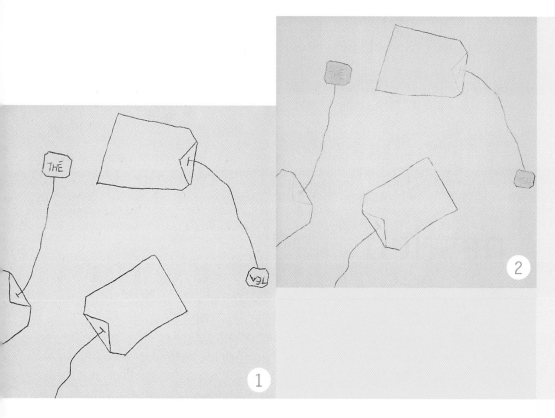

STEP 1 Paint the outside of the teapot and the entire cup with two coats of pale yellow. Transfer or copy the designs from page 110 on all sides in a random pattern. Technique is demonstrated on a tile here to better show fine detail.

STEP 2 Apply two coats of beige on the inside of each teabag. Paint the top folds of the teabags with three coats of beige to make them realistically darker. Paint each tag a different color, using two coats of mint, periwinkle, or peach. Let the paint dry completely.

tip

To simplify the process, transfer the tea bag pattern but not the string or tag. Then, draw in the strings and tags freehand. Don't forget: pencil lines will disappear during the firing process, so don't worry about mistakes.

STEP 3 With a thin liner brush, paint in the strings and outline the tea bags and tags with black. Paint the word TEA on the tags or the names of your favorite varieties.

VARIATION

White, which enhances soft colors, is used here to create a daisy-like flower pattern. Paint a grid over the entire teapot with two coats of periwinkle. Then paint the grid's squares using two coats of mint, peach and/or pale yellow as seen here. Make sure the teapot's spout is within a square so that it can be painted with one color. Paint flowers with two coats of white in some of the squares and on the top of the teapot lid. Paint a pale yellow center in each flower.

PERIWINKLE

PEACH

MINT

PALE YELLOW

special occasion PLATES

MATERIALS

- #4 round brush or ½" flat brush
- thin liner brush
- pencil
- ceramic paint underglaze colors: periwinkle, beige, peach, pale yellow, mint, lavender, white, black

Commemorative plates are the perfect outlet for a painter's creativity. Whether for a wedding, birth, graduation, anniversary, or other special event, the understated elegance of soft colors provides all the variety necessary to create tasteful, fun, personalized projects. The nearly flat surface allows maximum flexibility and ease in executing your designs, so don't be afraid to try something challenging.

STARTING OUT
Take a look at stamps from different countries to glean ideas for personalizing this project. Stamps come in many different shapes and perforation styles, and the wide variety can inspire unusual designs.

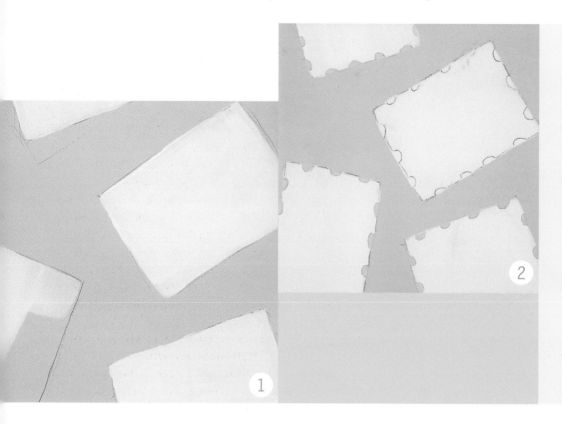

STEP 1 Using a wide, flat brush, apply two coats of periwinkle over the entire plate, front and back. When completely dry, pencil in several rectangular shapes in a random pattern. With a round or flat brush, apply two good coats of white in the rectangles.

STEP 2 Pencil in a scalloped border around the white rectangles, using a postage stamp as a guide or the patterns on page 111. Draw a smaller inner rectangle within the stamps to create a border. Paint the scallops with two coats of periwinkle.

tip

Underglaze pencil smudges easily, so be careful not to handle the plate too much once this step is completed. (See variation.)

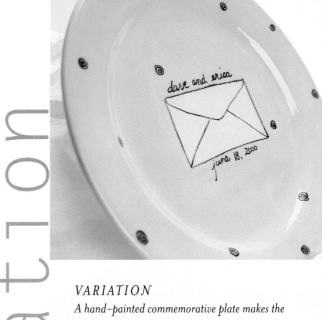

STEP 3 Paint the inside of the stamp with one solid coat of beige. Using a liner brush, paint a thin black line over the penciled border. Personalize the plate by painting images in the stamps that pertain to a special place, person, or event that you wish to commemorate. Use the other colors from the soft color palette for the images you choose. Be sure to include a postage amount in the lower right hand corner of the stamp to realistically complete the stamps. See page 111 for patterns.

variation

VARIATION

A hand-painted commemorative plate makes the perfect wedding gift for your favorite couple. To create the design seen here, begin by mixing a small amount of white into pale yellow and paint the entire plate twice. A wide, flat brush allows for quick and even coating. Transfer the envelope pattern on page 111 to the middle of the plate. Paint the envelope with two coats of white. You should still be able to see the lines, but if not, you can re-transfer them or go over them with a pencil. Next, paint random dots using mint, lavender, and peach. Next, use a fine liner brush to add black spirals in each dot when completely dry. Then, with a pencil, hand-write the names of the couple at the top of the envelope and the wedding date under the envelope to give it the feel of a real handwritten letter. Carefully go over these with black paint. When all the paint is dry, outline the envelope with a black underglaze pencil.

PEACH

PALE YELLOW

MINT

LAVENDER

dessert
PLATES

Pastel hues and dimensional paint combine to create the iced-cake finish of this plate. Special desserts will get the attention they deserve when framed by a soothing, soft color. Since the specialty underglaze used to make the dotted pattern comes in handy squeeze bottles, perfect circles and lines are easy to achieve. Try experimenting with different bottle tops or cake decorating nibs for a variety of effects.

MATERIALS

- **#3 or #4 round brush**
- **thin liner brush**
- **pencil or carbon paper**
- **ceramic paint underglaze colors: light pink, mint, pale yellow, peach, black, white dimensional paint**

STARTING OUT

Remember always to add relief patterns last so that you don't smudge them while painting elsewhere. Practice making even-sized dots before painting them on the plate to avoid having to remove mistakes. Mistakes can be removed using a craft knife.

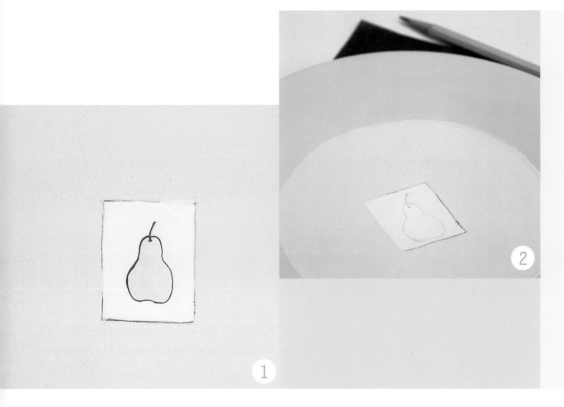

STEP 1 Draw a square or a rectangle in the center of the plate with a pencil. Draw the pear design from page 112 in the center of the rectangle.

STEP 2 Paint the inner circle of the plate with three coats of light pink, carefully avoiding the rectangle. Paint the outer circle and the underside of the plate with three coats of mint. Paint the pear with three coats of pale yellow. Let each coat dry completely before applying the next one. While the final coat of pale yellow is still damp, apply one coat of highlights with peach. When all the paint is dry, use a thin liner brush to outline the pear with one coat of black. For an impressionistic effect, try using only one or two coats of paint.

tip

Skip a step when transferring patterns by using graphite paper rather than cutting out and tracing templates. The lines will burn off in the kiln just like pencil markings.

VARIATION 1

Transfer the large pear design from page 112 to the center of your dessert plate. Paint the pear with three coats of pale yellow, and paint the leaf with three coats of mint. While the final coat of pale yellow is still damp, paint the edges of the pear with peach. Paint the outer circle of the plate with three coats of peach. Use a thin liner brush to outline the pear and to add the pear's stem with one coat of black. Finally, dip the blunt end of a brush into mint paint and dab dots on the plate rim.

MINT   PALE YELLOW   PEACH

STEP 3 Squeeze a pattern of dots onto the outer circle of the plate using white dimensional paint. Here, equally spaced dots outline the inside and outside edges of the mint circle.

LIGHT PINK

MINT

PALE YELLOW

PERIWINKLE

VARIATION 2

Try different motifs with a food theme such as the mug or utensils seen here. Draw your own designs or use the patterns on page 112.

sponged
SWITCH PLATE

A common household element like this switch plate offers a quick and easy way to add the finishing touch to a room. A simple design utilizing soft colors will add to the ambiance while not detracting from other decorative items and furnishings. And a room with textured, faux-finished walls deserves to have a coordinated switch plate. The mottled effect of sponging serves to soften muted colors even more, enhancing the understated appeal of the classic harlequin pattern used here.

MATERIALS

- **household sponges**
- **ceramic paint underglaze colors: periwinkle, lavender, mint, pale yellow**

STARTING OUT
Create a custom diamond-shaped sponge for this project by tracing the switch plate on graph paper and sketching out the pattern. Once you have determined the size of the diamonds, cut a diamond out of the graph paper, utilizing this template to create a perfectly geometric, diamond-shaped sponge stamp.

STEP 1 Sponge the switch plate with one coat of periwinkle and let it dry completely. Sponge one coat of lavender, and let it dry completely. See "Sponging" on page 76.

STEP 2 Sponge diamonds across the switch plate with one coat of mint, beginning in the upper left corner. Continue with the next row, being sure to align the bottom points of the completed diamonds with the tip of the sponge.

tip
Use a brush to load the perfect amount of paint on the sponge for a clear, complete image.

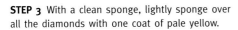

3

STEP 3 With a clean sponge, lightly sponge over all the diamonds with one coat of pale yellow.

VARIATION

Use a thin liner brush to paint spirals within some of the diamonds, or choose a motif from your home. This single-switch plate has a pale yellow base coat. The diamonds were sponged with beige, followed by peach. The spirals were also painted in peach.

PALE YELLOW

BEIGE

PEACH

favorite**soft**colors
Color and Painting Workshop

working with
soft colors

The understated colors of this palette can be combined and layered in ways that would be undesirable or ineffective with darker or brighter colors. Muted enough so that they complement rather than overpower each other, these hues can be thrown together freely to elicit subtle, yet interesting combinations.

A design using lots of colors or bold images can be subdued or unified by covering the whole piece with one thin layer of a soft color, creating a subtle patina to the piece. Alternatively, painting over a soft color background will only slightly modify the top color.

White paint, which would normally become diluted and indistinct when applied over other colors, can be used to create beautifully ethereal designs when applied over soft colors. There is no need to rely on the natural color of the ceramic form to work white into a design when using this palette!

Finally, display softly colored projects in rooms with a lot of natural light or white walls to accentuate the pieces.

Two coats of white over an opaque background result in a distinct but translucent and airy look.

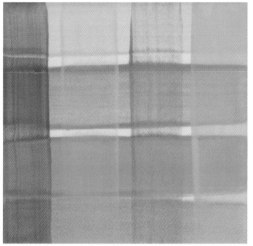

This overlapping design uses all the colors of this palette. The result is a plaid motif that is fun and appealing, but not overwhelming.

mixing soft colors

The soft color palette with its wide range of colors offers great flexibility for color mixing. Since the muted nature of the colors allows them to be overlapped and layered freely, experimental color mixing is sure to yield successful results.

Mixing two colors will yield predictable new colors. For example, pink and yellow combine to create an orange hue. In addition to straightforward combinations, try mixing several colors in varying amounts. Slightly adjusting a hue with small amounts of other paints can create a whole palette of closely related colors, great for adding details and depth to a painting project. You can create several shades of the same color by even slightly adjusting the ratio of the paints being mixed and using this range of related colors to capture the shades of realistic tones.

Remember, unfired colors will look dry and pale, but the fired version will be a richer, brighter, deeper hue. For an even color, mix the paints thoroughly.

Another interesting technique is marbling. Begin with a saucer or cup filled with one color. Then, swirl one or more colors into the paint, being sure not to blend the colors completely. A squeeze bottle is ideal for adding the additional colors, and a thin stick will help create a marbled pattern without completely blending the colors. When brushed on a ceramic piece, the mixture will create an interesting free-form pattern of semi-blended colors.

Equal parts of peach and pale yellow create a muted melon hue.

Equal parts of pink and lavender create an elegant dusty rose.

sponging

Sponges are available in a wide variety of textures and shapes, making them invaluable for creating patterns and layering colors. Sponges can quickly cover ceramic surfaces and blend colors easily, producing a professional, natural look.

Cut sponges into shapes like circles, squares, trees, or stars to make a set of sponge stamps. First, make a cardboard template of the shape; then cut it out and trace it on the sponge. By using the same stamp to layer different colors of paint, you can create images with lovely variations and depth of color. Compressed sponges, sold at craft stores and hardware stores, are especially useful for making sponge stamps. They are sold flat, so you can easily draw on them with markers and cut them into shapes with scissors.

Always dampen sponges before using them to make them more flexible and absorbent, but be sure to squeeze out excess water so that the paint isn't diluted. To control the amount of paint, use a flat brush to load the sponge. This also ensures that the sponge is evenly covered, which is especially important when sponging shapes. Too much paint can create too thick a layer of paint and will obscure the pattern of the sponge. Too little will produce a shape that may not be distinct enough.

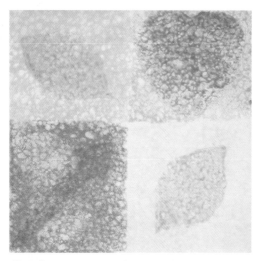

Shaped sponges are used to stamp images over a sponged background, creating the patterns seen here. The resulting delicate, lacy look is well suited to soft colors.

Light blue has been sponged over purple in the tile seen here. At the top, the colors have been sponged loosely and unevenly, creating a pattern with lots of variation and keeping each color distinct. At the bottom, the sponging is dense and even, blending the colors more and thereby creating a more uniform pattern.

specialty underglazes

A number of specialty paints that grant even more artistic opportunities for painting pottery are available to the modern ceramist. Often available at pottery studios, they can create fun, unusual, and unexpected results that add an interesting twist to decorated ceramics.

One of these specialty paints is a dimensional paint, variously called 'bumpy', 'stand-up', or 'puff' paint, which creates lines, dots, and other patterns that remain dimensional after firing. This modern product has its roots in the traditional technique called slip trailing, which utilizes a thick but liquid clay called 'slip' to create patterns. Since it is not brushed on, dimensional paint, sold in squeeze bottles, is easily applied to ceramic surfaces. By adjusting the amount of pressure applied to the bottle, you can produce lines of various widths and symmetrical dots of different sizes. Try dragging a thin tool such as a toothpick through the wet paint to create a feathered look or painting smaller dots on top of larger dots using two different colors.

Underglaze pencils, which work just like regular lead pencils, are also available at many painting studios. Writing words and drawing pictures on ceramics can result in some beautiful work that will have friends and family wondering how you did it! Try tracing cut-outs and signing your work or adding text to a piece. Outlining with a brush requires a steady hand, so outlining with underglaze pencils provides an easier option. Since the pencils smudge easily, use them last so that you avoid handling the piece too much.

Raised dots and lines are easy to make with dimensional paints, creating a fun, tactile finish.

Underglaze pencils, available in a variety of colors, add an appealing, handwritten feel that is impossible to create with a brush.

The rich, warm colors that make up this palette come from the earth itself. Earth colors hearken back to times when pigments came from nature, and they add a classical flair to hand-painted ceramics.

favorite**earth**colors

Always welcoming and inviting, this palette should be used when you want to bring the lush tones of the outdoors to your home. Use this earth color palette to create a Tuscan mood. Or use it to glaze cups and mugs designed for celebrating with friends and family. The meals you prepare from your garden's harvest will look even more appetizing when presented on hand-painted dishware.

These earth-inspired colors of leaf, fruit, soil, and stream are also the perfect complements to ceramic forms that are intimately linked with nature. Use them outdoors on planters or any other practical or decorative items. Use them indoors, especially on pots that will hold your favorite flowers and houseplants.

tuscan espresso
CUP & SAUCER

MATERIALS

- #4 or #5 round brush
- thin liner brush
- pencil
- ceramic paint underglaze colors: tan, burnt orange, light green, black

Earth colors are the intuitive choice for this cup and saucer, designed to serve rich, steaming espresso—of an earthy color itself. To create a truly unique set, use the same motif on each piece, but experiment with different color combinations within the earth palette. You will end up with cups and saucers that are definitely coordinated, but don't imitate each other. The professionally crisp yet fluid lines of the leaf are easy to create yourself. An easy-to-cut template on page 113 and an ordinary pencil ensure consistent results.

STARTING OUT The bottom of this cup and the inner circle of the saucer are painted the same color to visually unify the two pieces. As a final step, outlining in black where colors meet ensures a neat separation between them.

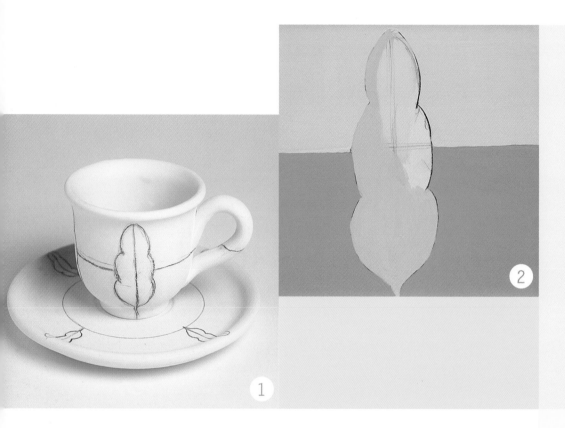

STEP 1 Pencil a circle in the center of the saucer. Then, draw a line around the circumference of the cup, dividing it into two approximately equal parts. Cut out the leaf templates on page 113. Trace the larger leaf three times randomly around the cup with a pencil. Trace the smaller leaf four times on the saucer, with each leaf opposite another. Don't worry about erasing pencil lines and smudges, as they will burn off during firing.

STEP 2 Avoiding the leaf shape outline, apply three coats of tan to the top half of the cup and the outer circle of the saucer. Apply three coats of burnt orange to the bottom half of the cup and the inner circle of the saucer. Let each coat dry completely before applying the next one. Be careful to avoid the leaf outlines. Next, paint inside the leaves with light green. For opaque leaves, use three coats; for a transparent wash, use one or two coats.

tip

To keep the color of the leaves true, be careful not to overlap the light green with any of the other colors.

tip

If you make a mistake, don't worry. When the underglaze has dried, you can scrape away the mistake with a craft knife.

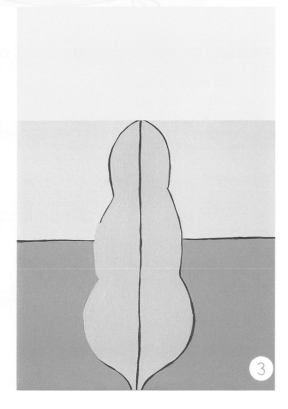

STEP 3 Outline the leaves, the inner circle on the saucer, and the line that divides the top and bottom of the cup with one coat of black using a thin liner brush. Paint a line down the middle of each leaf, sketching it in first with a pencil if desired.

variations

VARIATION 1
Use different earth tones to create a set of unique but complementary pieces. Here, brown was used in place of burnt orange.

TAN BROWN LIGHT GREEN

VARIATION 2
An alternate palette and improvised details can be added to complete the set.

BURNT ORANGE TUSCAN BLUE LIGHT GREEN

favorite earth colors 83

leaf & vine
SERVING PLATTER

The earthy garland framing this platter is intended to surround culinary creations, and the natural motif makes it perfect for serving homegrown food. The realistically shaded vine stands out when painted on a non-competitive but contrasting white background. The autumnal yellow and orange border enhances any dish prepared from the pick of a bountiful harvest.

MATERIALS

- **#3 or #4 round brush**
- **thin liner brush**
- **graphite paper**
- **pencil**
- **ceramic paint underglaze colors: Tuscan blue; burnt orange; deep yellow; black**

STARTING OUT To keep the scallops consistent in a freely drawn border, try sketching rough guidelines on the platter. Begin by drawing lines down the vertical and horizontal midpoints. Then divide the rest of the space like a pie.

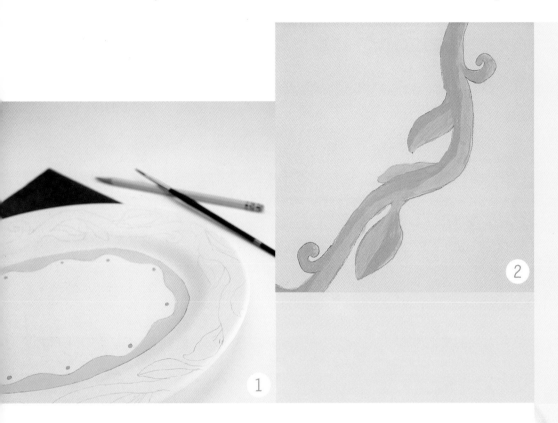

STEP 1 Using graphite paper, transfer the vine pattern on pages 116 & 117 to the outer edge of the platter. Pencil in a line around the inside of the platter, following the ridge. Draw a scalloped border freehand about 1" away from the previous pencil line. Apply three coats of deep yellow between the two lines. Let each coat dry completely before applying the next one. When the coats are completely dry, dip the handle end of your brush in burnt orange and mark a dot within each scallop of the border. Apply enough paint to make a solid, even dot.

STEP 2 Paint the vine with two coats of Tuscan blue and deep yellow, mixed in equal proportions. Before the second coat is dry, paint one coat of deep yellow highlights on one side of each leaf and on one side of the vine.

tip
For a more realistic look, paint highlights with a loose rather than a sharp, clean edge.

STEP 3 Using a thin liner brush, paint veins on the leaves and outline the vine, leaves, and border with one coat of black.

VARIATION 1

The wide scalloped border on the edge of this platter dips into the bottom to create the impression that the platter, itself, is wavy. To create this pattern, begin by drawing a scalloped border free-hand. Using a 1" or 2" wide flat brush, paint the border with two coats of light green. Paint the inside bottom of the platter with three coats of tan. Paint the outer edge with three coats of burnt orange. When the paint is completely dry, dip the handle end of your brush in dark brown and mark dots around both wavy lines. To make smaller dots within the brown dots, dip a pencil tip in light green, or burnt orange as seen here.

TAN	LIGHT GREEN
BURNT ORANGE	BROWN

VARIATION 2

To create the oak leaf border on this platter, transfer the pattern on page 113. Here, moss green and deep yellow leaves are set against a burnt orange background for a festive fall platter.

MOSS GREEN	BURNT ORANGE	DEEP YELLOW

green pepper
GARDEN MARKER

This permanent, visual marker is a creative alternative to the purely functional kind found in gardens. To design markers for other vegetables or flowers in your garden, consult food related clip art books. If you have trouble finding any of the pictures you need, try tracing the photo on a seed package to create a simple line drawing.

MATERIALS

- #3 or #4 round brush
- thin liner brush
- graphite paper
- pencil
- ceramic paint underglaze colors: light green, deep yellow, moss green, black

STARTING OUT

When marking the border for this project, if the total number of spaces is even, a checkered pattern of alternating colors will work out properly. Mark each corner first; then mark off the spaces between each corner.

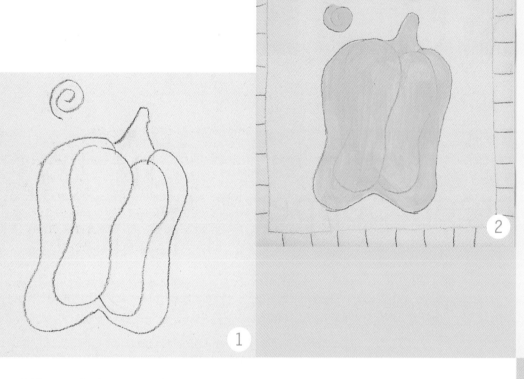

STEP 1 Transfer the pepper and spiral patterns on page 115 to the marker.

STEP 2 Draw a border around the pepper about ½" in from the edge of the marker, and then divide the border into squares to create a checkerboard pattern. Paint the pepper with one coat of light green, and paint over the spiral with one coat of deep yellow. The pencil line underneath should still be visible as a guide for outlining.

tip

To make this pepper look realistic, two shades of green are used to simulate the effect of light on the curved surface. Use a lighter shade for areas that are prominent, such as the bumps of the pepper, and darker shades for areas that are recessed, such as the grooves of the pepper.

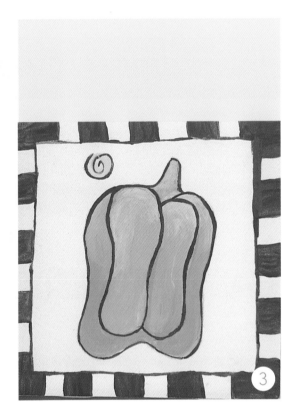

VARIATION

What's a garden without flowers? Instead of a traditional border, stylized leaves frame this blossom, creating a dynamic union of form and design. First, transfer the tulip pattern on page 115 to the center of the marker. Dip the brush in moss green and then in light green. Paint the leaves and stem with one coat of this mixture. Painting with two colors at once produces a quick and easy blended effect. Be sure to follow the line of the pattern when painting, as brush strokes will be visible in the fired marker. Color in the tulip with three coats of brick red. Using a thin liner brush, outline everything with one coat of black.

LIGHT GREEN   MOSS GREEN   BRICK RED

STEP 3 Using a thin liner brush, paint over the pencil lines of the pepper with one coat of black. Apply one coat of moss green over the pepper, but not over the outlines. Apply a second coat of moss green along the pencil outlines to add dimension. When the paint is completely dry, add light green highlights to the bumps of the pepper. Using a thin liner brush, apply one coat of black over the pencil lines of the spiral. Fill in every other space of the checkered border with one coat of black.

variation

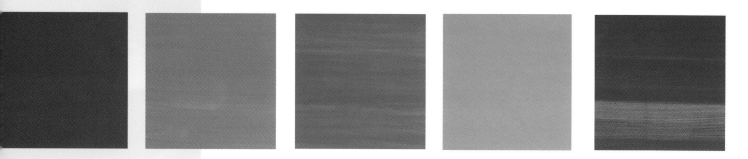

terracotta
PASTA BOWLS

These individual pasta bowls are painted on terracotta rather than on white bisqueware. The rich, naturally reddish-brown clay adds an extra dimension of earthy color. Terracotta is widely used by potters in countries such as Mexico, Spain, Greece, and Italy. When earth palette colors are set against this darker background rather than a white one, they give these colors a warmer feeling, making them welcome at the dinner table.

MATERIALS

- flat brush
- thin liner brush
- compressed sponges or household sponges
- ceramic paint underglaze colors: moss green, light green, burnt orange, deep yellow, brown

STARTING OUT
There are many ceramic forms that can be used to make these individual pasta bowls. Choose one that suits your style, as well as your appetite!

STEP 1 Using a jar or bottle to trace around, pencil in a circle inside on the bottom of the bowl. Draw another line around the circle, about 1" away from it. Now, draw a line around the inside of the bowl about ½" to ¾" down from the edge. Then, draw a line around the middle of the bowl on the outside. Paint the inside inner circle of the bowl with three coats of light green. Using a flat brush, paint the inside outer circle with three coats of burnt orange. Using a thin liner brush, paint over the line ½" to ¾" from the edge of the bowl with deep yellow. Painting the center of the bowl first and then working outward helps you from accidentally smudging the wet areas of paint. Turn the bowl over and paint three coats of light green on the outside lower half.

tip
Compressed sponges can be drawn on and easily cut into shapes because they are flat until submerged in water.

2

VARIATION
The white clay bowl seen here was painted with the same colors and techniques used on the terracotta bowls, but the result is a much brighter look.

MOSS GREEN

LIGHT GREEN

BURNT ORANGE

DEEP YELLOW

BROWN

STEP 2 Cut a thin oval-shaped leaf from either a compressed sponge or an ordinary kitchen sponge. Dampen the sponge, and then paint half the oval with moss green and the other half with light green. Press the sponge in a random pattern on the inside of the bowl, alternating the angle of the leaves. Paint the outside of the bowl in the same way. When all the paint is dry, use a liner brush to paint the stems with brown.

favorite**earth**colors
Color and Painting Workshop

color
intensity

A variety of effects can be achieved using a single underglaze color, from a shimmering translucent wash to bold, even coverage. Brushstrokes can be made very visible or hardly visible, depending on how many layers of the color you apply. Try experimenting with different-sized brushes and sponges to achieve depth and texture, or applying an underglaze unevenly to combine these effects.

A range of values is also possible by simply adding more layers of the same underglaze: each will have its own characteristics, so experiment with the range of each color you will be working with for a project. Try creating your own reference tiles by painting stripes of one, two, three, and four layers of the same color. These portable swatches will help you plan and design your projects at home.

Finally, when painting on white bisqueware, keep in mind that any areas that you don't paint will fire shiny white. This is the true color of the clay, which becomes shiny because of the clear glaze that is applied over the whole piece before firing.

A single coat of underglaze will fire pale and translucent; this is especially true of blue underglazes. The resulting effect is a pleasing watercolor wash.

Two coats of underglaze intensify colors and highlight brushstrokes, adding a handcrafted, folksy style to the design.

To obtain the most intense color and to minimize visible brushstrokes, use three or more coats of underglaze. The resulting flat, even coverage complements bold graphic designs such as stripes.

blending
colors

Blending colors adds dimension and detail and provides a wide array of decorating possibilities. Discover just what effects you can achieve by experimenting with as many combinations as you can think of within your palette.

Blending can be barely noticeable—just enough to add a hint of depth—or can be used to join two contrasting colors with a soft and blurry edge rather than with a sharp line. The effect depends on how closely related the colors are, how heavily you apply the final color, and whether the base coat is wet or dry when you apply highlights.

Highlights added before the base coat is completely dry will blend easily and naturally. The wetter the base coat is, the more the paints will blend and the subtler and softer the effect will be. To brighten highlights, add a layer of paint after the first one has dried. To keep highlight colors distinct, apply them to a completely dry base coat.

This leaf is painted with light green only, creating a flat, graphic look.

For a more realistic leaf, shade deep yellow on top of light green, following the outline of half of the leaf. Outline everything in black to accentuate the design.

Introduce a third, darker color for depth, contrast, and a very detailed, realistic effect. Here, deep yellow and brown are shown on opposite sides of a light green leaf.

layering colors

Underglaze colors can be softened and muted by layering. This is a great technique to use for pieces requiring subtle color changes or for creating a variegated background effect. Try layering several different colors, reversing the order of the colors, or applying multiple layers of the same color over another color to see how the colors modify each other.

Many earth-palette colors are of the same medium tone, making it easy to layer them with pleasing results. However, it's best not to layer them at all if you want to maintain a sharp edge or to keep distinct an image that you have already painted. To soften edges but still keep colors distinct, overlap underglazes only at the point where colors meet.

When layering different colors, the top color will become muted, as is this light green when applied over burnt orange.

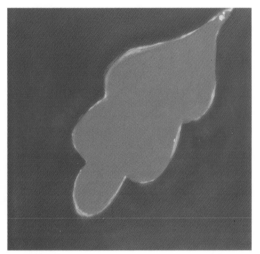

Here, light green stays crisp and true because the background color is carefully painted around it to avoid any overlap.

mixing colors

To expand color selection without leaving the main palette, mix underglazes before applying them. You can create your own unique colors by simply experimenting and creating color mixing "recipes." Mixing underglazes works the same as with many other paints–yellow and blue make green, for example. However, unfired colors differ greatly in hue from the finished color, so it is impossible to tell what your green will look like until you fire it. Create color "test tiles" as handy visual references for ceramic painting.

Keep track of the colors you have mixed with notes about the results or a fired sample tile so that you don't duplicate your experiments. And don't forget to record recipes in a journal as you work—especially the percentages of one color to another—so that any successes can be easily duplicated. To eliminate guesswork, write the finished recipe on the back of your fired sample tiles.

Equal parts deep yellow and Tuscan blue create the rich green shown in the center of this tile.

Equal parts of tan and brick red result in this peachy salmon color.

templates

Preparing Templates

To use the templates in this book, start by determining the pattern size needed. The easiest way to do this is by photocopying the selected template and experimenting with reducing or enlarging the image to discover a size that works with a particular ceramic form.

Depending on the project, the template can be made from paper, adhesive vinyl, or thin, flexible cardboard. If a pattern will be used often, make it out of cardboard so that it can be reused several times. For very curved surfaces, paper or adhesive vinyl is a better choice. Adhesive vinyl is the best choice for masking out areas, especially if keeping within lines is a concern.

To transfer the properly sized, photocopied pattern to a piece of cardboard, simply cut it out and trace it; then use a craft knife or scissors to cut the cardboard. For more complex patterns with interior lines, graphite transfer paper, available at art and craft supply stores, works best. To use graphite paper, there is no need to cut out the template; transfer will be a matter of tracing. To transfer the pattern to a piece of adhesive vinyl, cut out the pattern from a piece of paper and trace it using a permanent marker.

Using Templates

To transfer a paper or cardboard pattern to a ceramic form, first wipe the piece free of dust with a damp sponge; let it dry. Next, use masking tape to hold the pattern in place. Then, using a #2 pencil, trace around the paper or cardboard image. To transfer more complex images with interior lines, such as the one used for the Green Pepper Garden Marker project on page 88, use a piece of graphite paper. Simply position the photocopy on the ceramic piece, place the graphite underneath it, and trace over the pattern lines. You can use masking tape to hold the pattern in place. Both pencil lines and graphite transfer lines will burn off in the kiln, so there is no need to erase them or worry about covering them completely.

When using a paper cutout, try misting it with a spray bottle and gently applying it to the ceramic surface to hold it in place. Paint over the cutout and remove it with a craft knife when the paint is dry. Touch up the edges if necessary with a thin brush. Paint inside the outline or leave it unpainted.

Templates can be used not only to provide painting guidelines, but also to create a number of unique effects. Try sponging, brushing, or spattering paint around a template to leave the silhouette of the image. A cutout template often leaves an interesting "negative." This "negative" can be used in conjunction with the "positive" cutout to layer colors, or it can be saved to use on a completely different project. Finally, try combining patterns from different projects to come up with new designs.

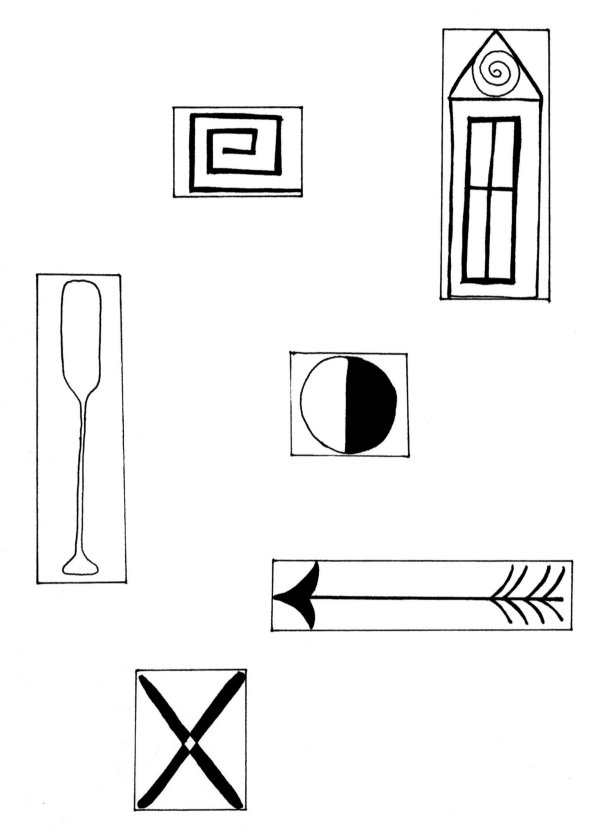

ILLUSTRATED MUGS

SALT AND PEPPER SHAKERS

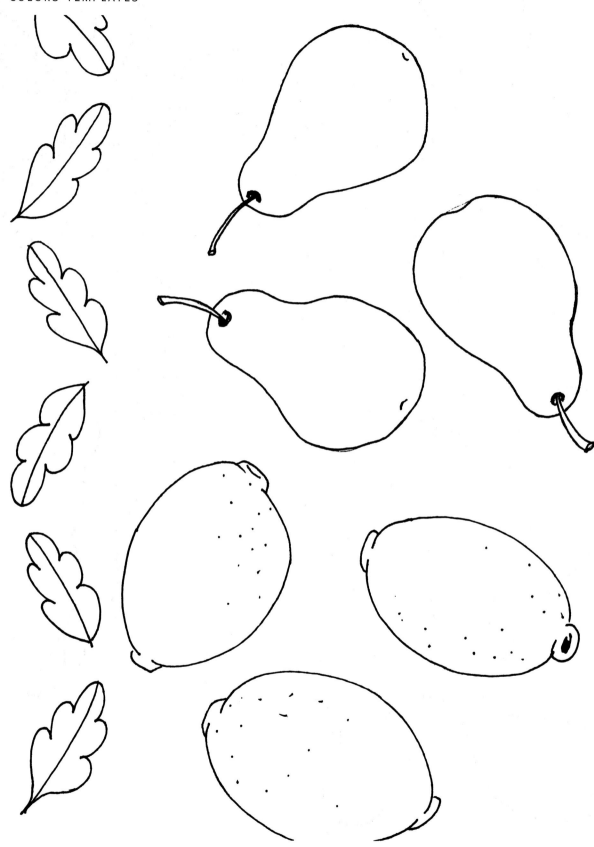

FRUIT PLATES

CHIP 'N DIP PARTY PLATTER

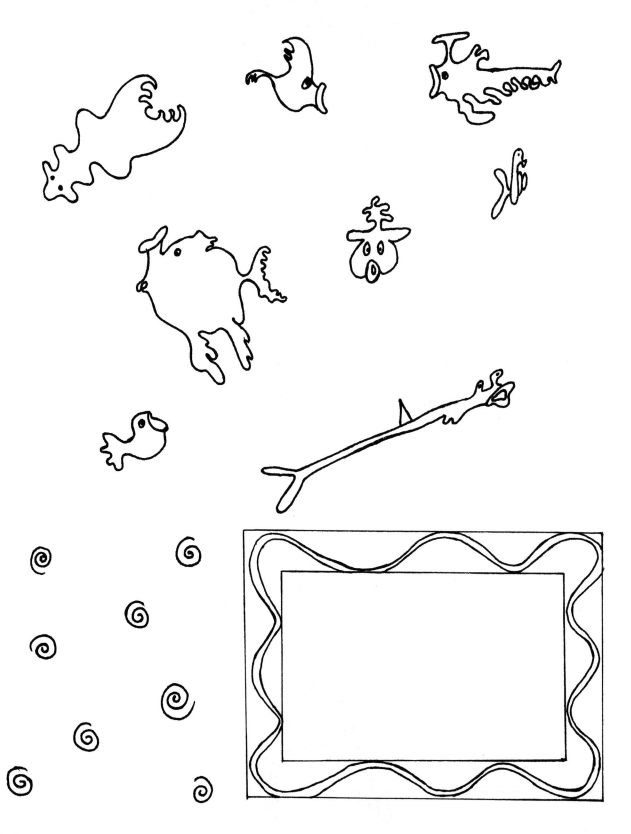

STAMPED SEA TILES

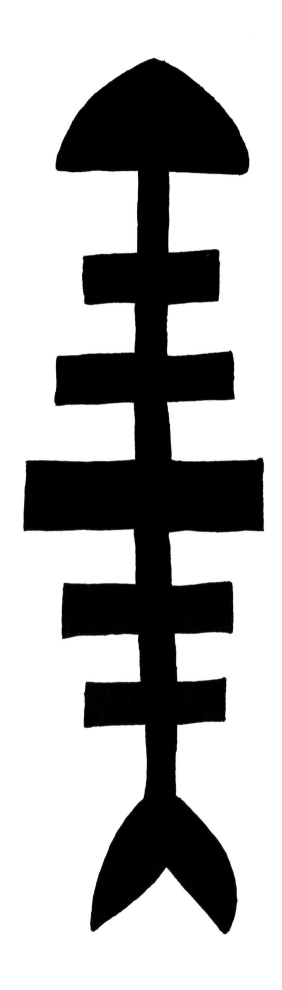

FISHBONE PLATTER

FISHBONE PLATTER FOR POSSIBLE VARIATION

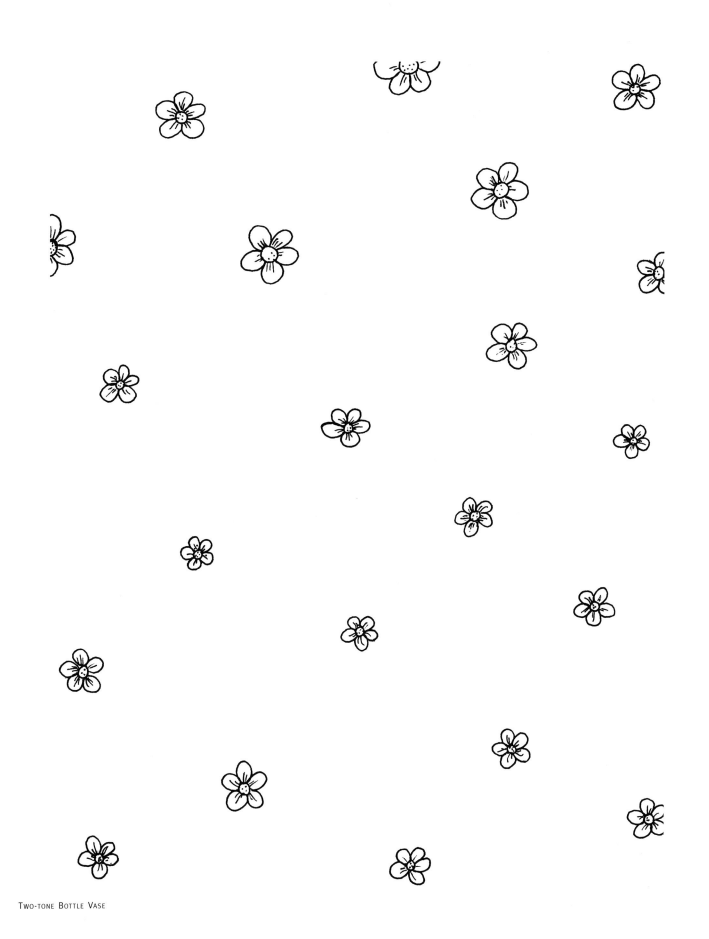

TWO-TONE BOTTLE VASE

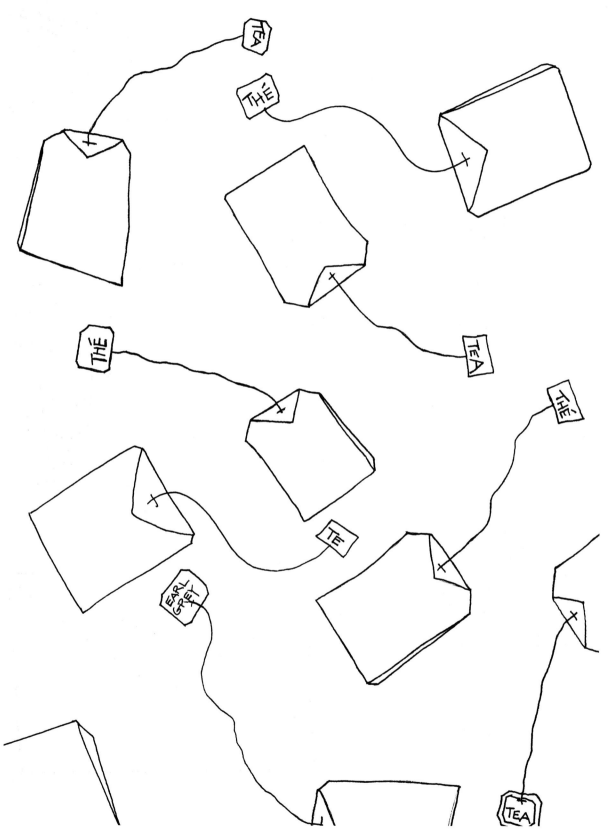

Nestled Teapot and Cup

SPECIAL OCCASION PLATE

DESSERT PLATES

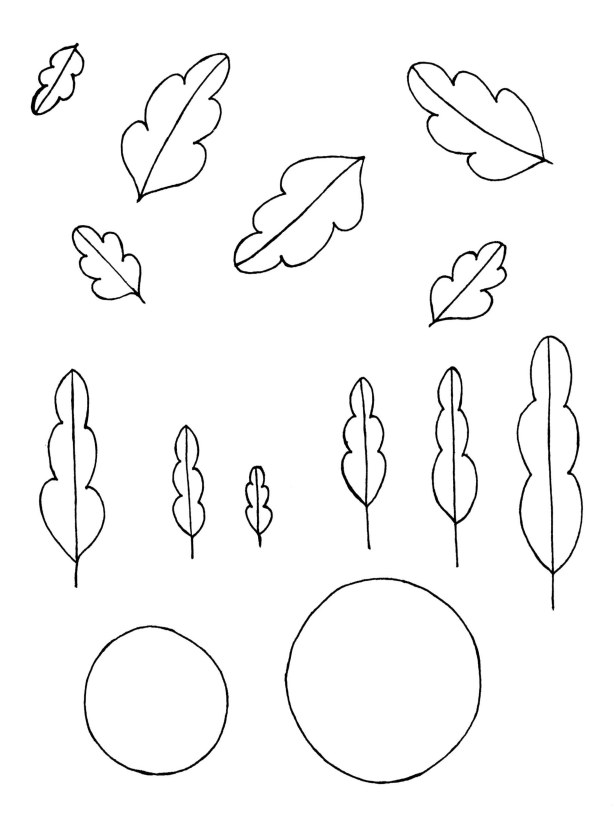

TUSCAN ESPRESSO SET

Terracotta Pasta Bowls Variations

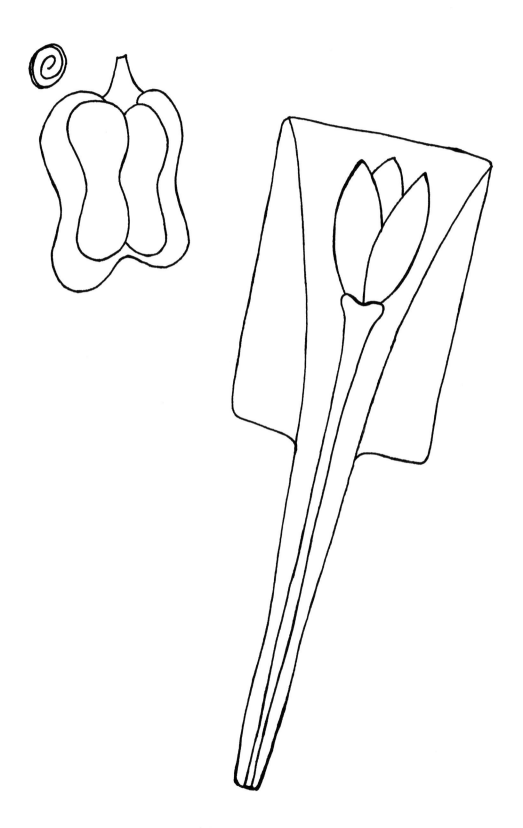

Green Pepper and Tulip Garden Markers

Leaf and Vine Serving Platter

RESOURCES

Paints:
Gare
165 Rosemount Street
Haverhill, MA 01831
978-373-9131
www.gare.com

Spectrum Glazes
P.O. Box 874
Lewiston, NY 14092
800-970-1970

Coloramics Distribution
4077 Weaver Court S.
Hilliard, OH 43026
614-876-1171
www.maycocolors.com
www.ceramichrome.com

Mayco
4077 Weaver Court South
Hilliard, OH 43026
614-876-1171
www.maycocolors.com

Duncan Enterprises
5673 East Shields Avenue
Fresno, CA 93727
www.duncanceramics.com

Ceramic Supplies:
(brushes, paint, craft supplies)
National Artcraft
7996 Darrow Road
Twinsburg, Ohio 44087
888-937-2723
www.nationalartcraft.com

Lou Davis Wholesale
Dept. PC 20, N3211 County Road H
PO Box 21
Lake Geneva, WI 53147-0021
800-748-7991

Red Barn Ceramics
Rt 13 South
Cortland, NY 13045
800-640-2039
www.ceramichrome.com

Corey Ceramic Supply
87 Messina Drive
Braintree, MA 02184
800-876-2776

Tiles:
HBD Ceramics
P.O. Box 910
Leland, MI 49854
231-386-7977

Bisqueware:
Bisque USA
P.O. Box 23963
Columbus, Ohio 43223
888-247-8729

Ceramic Supply of
New York and New Jersey
7 Route 46 West
Lodi, New Jersey 07644
800-7CERAMIC

Art Seasons
667 S. Hudson Avenue
Pasadena, CA 91106
888-354-9494
www.artseasons.com

Pull Cart
31 West 21st Street
New York, NY 10010
888-pulcart
mailto:pllcart@aol.com

Munsonville Clayworks
274 Murdough Hill Road
Munsonville, NH 03457
603-847-9767

Bisquefire
A division of Gare
Haverhill, MA 01831
888-292-0885
www.gare.com

Garrard Pottery
154 Andrew Drive
Suite 200
Stockbridge, GA 30281
800 335-3808
www.GarrardPottery.com

More Bisqueware:
Creative Touch
111 Lafayette Road Unit #4
P.O. Box 5291
Salisbury, MA 01952
978-462-2618
bisqueware, paints

BMW Bisque
225 Cash Street
Jacksonville, Texas 75766
800-388-2001
www.bmwbisque.com

Ceramica Imports
60 Spring Street, Suite 414
New York, New York 10012
888-424-7533

Alternative Wares
2749 Saturn Street
Brea, CA 92821
888-888-8247

Although you may use any brand of ceramic paint, the colors used throughout this book are manufactured by Gare. The color names appearing in [ ] are those of the manufacturer. Use this color reference guide when purchasing these paints from a Gare distributor.

FAVORITE BRIGHT COLORS

FAVORITE COOL COLORS

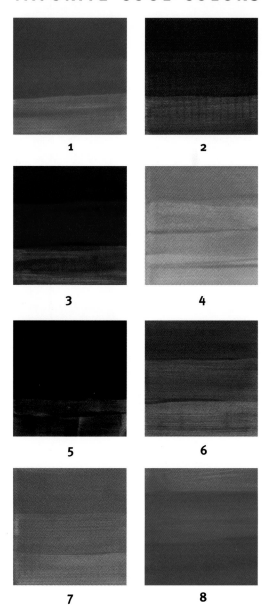

FAVORITE BRIGHT COLORS

1 bright yellow [smiley face]

2 lime green [lime rickey]

3 orange [orange peel]

4 honey yellow [yellow pencil]

5 apple red [lady bug]

6 deep orange [arriba]

7 aquamarine [jumpin' juniper]

8 turquoise [blue heaven]

FAVORITE COOL COLORS

1 aqua [jumpin' juniper]

2 purple [wineona]

3 royal blue [blue by you]

4 mint [hint o' mint]

5 deep blue-green [calypso]

6 grape [grape slush]

7 light blue [something blue]

8 turquoise [blue heaven]

FAVORITE SOFT COLORS

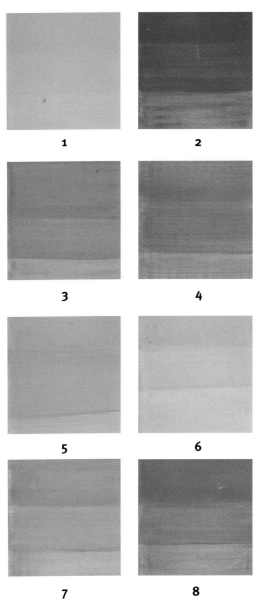

1 2

3 4

5 6

7 8

FAVORITE EARTH COLORS

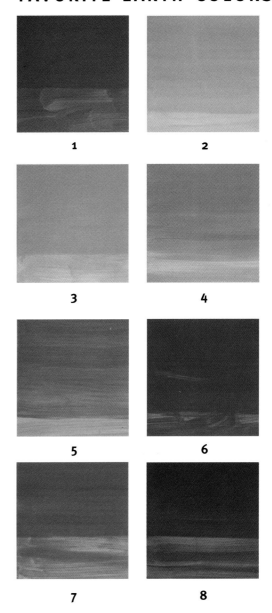

1 2

3 4

5 6

7 8

1 pale yellow [tweety bird]

2 pink [in the pink]

3 peach [peachy keen]

4 lavender [the color purple]

5 beige [naked truth]

6 light pink [this li'l piggy]

7 mint [hint o mint]

8 periwinkle [something blue]

1 moss green [mocha rose]

2 deep yellow [old yeller]

3 tan [butterscotch]

4 light green [leap frog]

5 burnt orange [Indian summer]

6 Tuscan blue [newt blue]

7 brick red [lady bug]

8 brown [chocolate mousse]

INDEX

ACKNOWLEDGMENTS

Many thanks to the following artists, colleagues, and friends who contributed their knowledge, skills, and time to this project:

For their design and painting contributions—Valeria Lanza, Linda Mastandrea, and Rose Seamens, to all the people at Paint a Plate Studio—Amy Robillard, Lesley Mottla, Melanie DeTeso, Phyllis Mottla, and Dara DiLiegro for their creative input and technical help. Thanks to Mae Lucas and Michelle Fino, painting assistants, and to Zach Wilshire, the kiln master. I'd also like to acknowledge the customers and friends I have made at Paint A Plate for their continuing artistic inspiration and support.

To those at Rockport Publishers for their contributions to the success of this project. I am most grateful to writer Livia McRee for her creativity, talented writing skills, and uncanny ability to make everything seem so effortless; to Martha Wetherill for finding me; to Shawna Mullen, my editor, for her vision, patience, encouragement, and her much appreciated sense of humor, which kept everything in perspective; to Judy Schurger for putting it all together; and to the talented design and editorial team, Regina Grenier, Silke Braun, and Kristy Mulkern.

Rockport Publishers gives special acknowledgment to Livia McRee for her contributions to the writing of this book.

ABOUT THE AUTHORS

Doreen Mastandrea received her MFA from Cranbrook Academy of Art in Michigan. She has taught a variety of courses in ceramics at Salem State College, Montserrat College of Art, the DeCordova Museum, and Mudflat Studios, among others. Her artwork has been shown across the country and in Canada. Currently, Doreen owns Paint A Plate Studio, a paint-your-own pottery shop in Lexington, Massachusetts.

Livia McRee is a craft writer and designer who has written and contributed to many books, including *The Crafter's Project Book, The Right Light, Paper House* (Rockport Publishers), and *Instant Fabic: Quilted Projects from Your Home Computer* (Martingale & Company).

DEDICATION

This book is dedicated to my family, especially my parents, Anne and William Mastandrea, for their love and support throughout all of my artistic endeavors. And finally, to my friends for their endless encouragement, especially to Cran, Linda, Michael, Harry, and Susan for being such great friends.